*"What is REAL?" asked the Rabbit one day, when they
were lying side by side near the nursery fender, before
Nana came to tidy the room. "Does it mean having things
that buzz inside you and a stick-out handle?"
"Real isn't how you are made," said the Skin Horse.
"It's a thing that happens to you."*
—from *The Velveteen Rabbit*, 1922

Becoming Real

THE TRUE STORY OF THE VELVETEEN RABBIT

Words by *Molly Golden* • Art by *Paola Escobar*

Clarion Books
An Imprint of HarperCollinsPublishers

Clarion Books is an imprint of HarperCollins Publishers.

Becoming Real: The True Story of the Velveteen Rabbit
Text copyright © 2025 by Molly Golden
Illustrations copyright © 2025 by Paola Escobar

For information address HarperCollins Children's Books, a division of
HarperCollins Publishers, 195 Broadway, New York, NY 10007.
www.harpercollinschildrens.com

Library of Congress Control Number: 2024005385
ISBN 978-0-35-868154-0

This book was made using brushes in Adobe Photoshop with the valuable help
of little Paola, eight years old, and her rabbit friend Copito de Nieve.
Typography by Celeste Knudsen
24 25 26 27 28 RTLO 10 9 8 7 6 5 4 3 2 1

First Edition

For my parents, who have always
believed in my imagination
—M.G.

For Copito de Nieve, my sweet rabbit and
adventure pal during my childhood, and for Flora,
who now accompanies and brightens my days
—P.E.

LONG AGO IN LONDON, there was a little girl who didn't go to school.

Her name was Margery.

While other children marched in lines and sat in classrooms,

Margery's father gave her imagination all the
room it needed to leap and soar.
Margery pulled big books off his shelves.
She traced wings, outlined paws, sketched ears.

As her scissors snipped, paper
scraps fluttered to the floor.
Like magic! Animals played in
the palm of her hand.

Margery read books.

She wrote stories.

And she created entire lands for
her toys on the nursery room floor.

*For nursery magic is very strange and wonderful,
and only those playthings that are old and wise and
experienced like the Skin Horse understand all about it.*

Then Margery's father died,
and sorrow cast its shadow over
her world.
    She couldn't escape her
sadness, not even in her
imagination.

"Does it hurt?" asked the Rabbit.
"Sometimes," said the Skin Horse, for he was always truthful.

Margery's family left London and traveled across the ocean to New York City.

It was there that Margery found a wild and wonderful park.

The animals Margery read about in her father's books were not only alive in her imagination.

The animals were real!

CENTRAL PARK

Before long, happiness returned.

Margery attended school.

And as she grew, her imagination did too.

Margery returned to London to write stories and published three novels.

But she wanted to write something different.
And at the time she did not know what that
something could be.

Margery soon married and started a family.
They settled in a Paris apartment they called
the Toy Cupboard Flat.

In no time, Margery was making paper toys for
her own children.

A boat set to sail. A tea kettle waiting for a party.

She watched her children's imaginations take flight—stacking, rocking, carrying their toys close.

. . . for the Boy used to talk to him, and made nice tunnels for him under the bedclothes that he said were like the burrows the real rabbits lived in. And they had splendid games together, in whispers . . .

But while her children played, nations went to war.

And the family needed a new home again.

Resources were scarce. The children were hungry. The family was cold.

So Margery encouraged her children to hold tight to their imaginations.

The children drew pictures
and created storybooks.
They played with their toys, by
now well-worn from adventure
and patched with love.

And together the family read.

. . . and the little Rabbit was very happy—so happy that he never noticed how his beautiful velveteen fur was getting shabbier and shabbier, and his tail becoming unsewn, and all the pink rubbed off his nose where the Boy had kissed him.

As the world emerged from battles, beaten and broken,
Margery returned to the land of her childhood.
And found joy.

Margery discovered
inspiration all around—

in a flower's petals,

a cupboard's creak,

the clattering of
forks in a drawer.

Everything had a story to tell,
especially the nursery room toys.

Margery thought of her children's
playthings:
   the rocking horse lined with rosettes,
   Petercat the teddy bear,
   a beautiful doll,
   the scuffed wooden dog.

Memories of her own childhood friends
filled her mind too.

Old Dobbin, the toy horse, frayed from
hours of adventure.
   Worn with wisdom.

She thought of her tattered old Tubby—
dingy with kisses and scruffy from cuddles.

With his wide eyes and
unusually long ears.

Ragged.
Loved.
Real.

What makes something real?

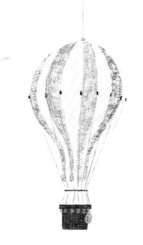

*. . . he scarcely looked like a rabbit anymore, except
to the Boy. To him he was always beautiful . . .*

Margery had been telling stories since she was a child.
Toys had always been a part of her life.
But could she share their story?

Margery had not written a book in a long time.
Perhaps she had forgotten how.

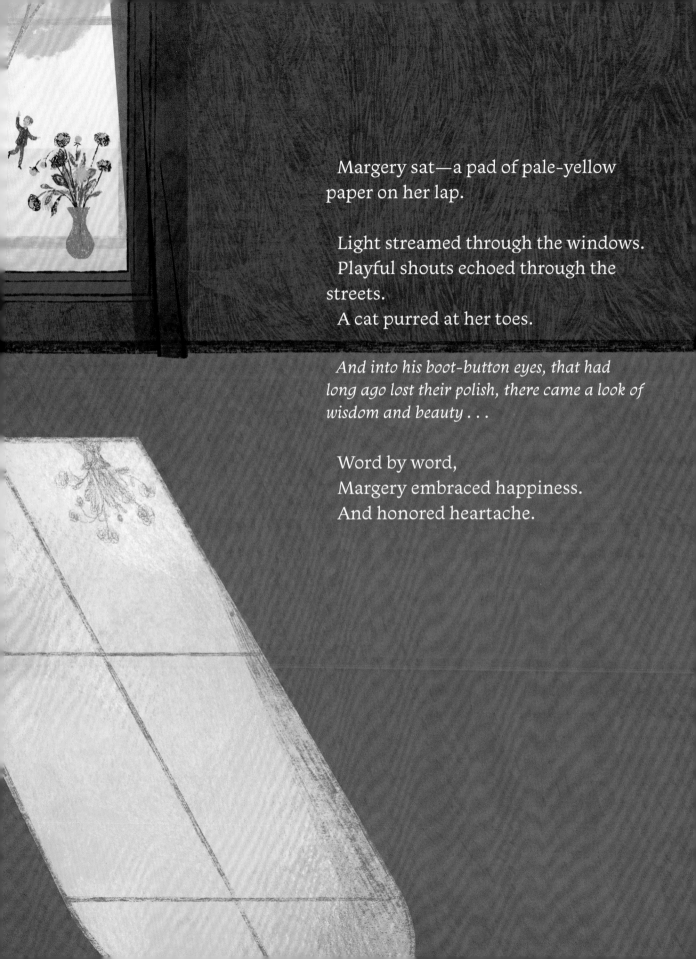

Margery sat—a pad of pale-yellow paper on her lap.

Light streamed through the windows. Playful shouts echoed through the streets.
A cat purred at her toes.

And into his boot-button eyes, that had long ago lost their polish, there came a look of wisdom and beauty . . .

Word by word,
Margery embraced happiness.
And honored heartache.

Like the seams of the old toy horse, Margery
stitched together a story about a rabbit whose
pink satin ears are rubbed gray and whose
whiskers wear off.
With his faded fur and shapeless body
—beautiful to his boy.

Margery wrote
of love,
of loss,
of becoming
real.

*. . . once you are Real you can't become
unreal again. It lasts for always.*

When Margery finished, she added a title.

The Velveteen Rabbit

A tale unlike any published for children before.

Soon, the Rabbit hopped in children's
imaginations around the world.
Made real through the power of love.

Brought to life as only Margery could.

After all, it was her story too.

"You were Real to the Boy," the Fairy said,
"because he loved you."

*Imagination is only another word for the
interpretation of life. It is through imagination that
a child makes his most significant contacts with
the world about him, that he learns tolerance, pity,
understanding, and the love for all created things.*

—MARGERY WILLIAMS BIANCO

Author's Note

MARGERY WILLIAMS WAS BORN IN LONDON IN 1881. She spent much of her early years alone reading and making up games. When she was still young, her father died, and her mother moved the family to New York City. Later the family moved to a farm in Pennsylvania, and Margery attended school for the first time, although her education was interrupted by frequent travel to England.

Margery returned to London to pursue writing and at age twenty-one published her first novel. She soon met and married bookseller Francesco Bianco. After their children, Cecco and Pamela, were born, Margery took a break from writing to focus on her young family. They lived in Paris for a time, but at the start of World War I, they packed up their toys and pets and moved to Italy. During the dark days of the war, Margery found fables, fairy tales, and poetry to be a source of hope. The stories and poems respected children's sorrow and embraced their joy. The writings gave Margery an appreciation of the timelessness of childhood.

After the war, Margery went back to New York City, this time with her own family. Margery was inspired to return to storytelling as she watched her children play with their own toys and pets. All the toys seemed so . . . real. In 1922, *The Velveteen Rabbit, or How Toys Become Real* was published.

Margery Williams Bianco died in 1944. *The Velveteen Rabbit* has remained in print around the world for more than a century, and through it, generations of children have found joy and learned what it means to be Real.

Social-Emotional Activities to Share with *Your* Toy

I HAD A SPECIAL TOY WHEN I WAS A CHILD—a little stuffed dog. After years of love, his fur is tattered, his ears have lost their stuffing, and his tail has been sewn back on many times. We had wonderful adventures together, but he was also a comfort to me when I was sad or scared or worried. Do you have a toy that is there for you in happy and sad times? Here are some activities you can share together!

- Curl up and listen to a story together. When you are ready, your stuffed animal can be your reading buddy, and you can read to them. You can also tell them stories you make up. Stuffed animals enjoy that.

- Have a picnic outside, just as the Boy did with the Velveteen Rabbit. You can invite a friend and their special toy too. I bet your toys become friends.

- Snuggle with your stuffed animal when it's raining outside and listen to the raindrops fall.

- Dress your stuffed animal in something they really want to wear. Maybe you can dress up to match!

- Eat pancakes together for breakfast . . . or lunch . . . or dinner.

- Toys are good listeners when you want to talk about something that is bothering you. Taking deep belly breaths and holding your stuffed animal close may help the worries fade too.

- Find somewhere for your toy to wait when you are gone. You can choose a special place or create one out of blankets or a shoebox. Mine would wait in my mother's purse. He even went grocery shopping once! Since I knew exactly where he was waiting for me, I felt less nervous when I was away.

- Start a journal with your toy. You and your stuffed animal can take turns writing or drawing what you each are thinking and how you are feeling.

- Make a natural habitat for your stuffed animal the way the Boy in *The Velveteen Rabbit* made burrows under his bedcovers for his Rabbit.

- Throw a birthday party for your toy. If you don't know their actual birth date, you can celebrate your "gotcha day"—the day your toy became yours forever.

- Make friends for you and your toy by tracing (or drawing), cutting, and folding animals the same way Margery made animals from her father's books.

Look for things that start with the same first letter as your toy's name. For example, if your stuffed animal's name is Daisy, you may find doors, daffodils, and dogs!

Draw a picture of you and your toy together in a place that holds a special memory for you or a place you would like to visit.

Host a stuffed animal parade with your friends and their stuffed animals. I'm sure the animals would like to take turns leading the way.

Dance together to your toy's favorite song. Your stuffed animal may not know how to dance, so you can show them some moves.

Bibliography

Banjo, Tayo. "Margery William Bianco." Pennsylvania Center for the Book, Penn State University Libraries, 2004, web.archive.org/web/20231101144446/pabook.libraries.psu.edu/literary-cultural-heritage-map-pa/bios/Bianco__Margery_Williams.

Bianco, Margery Williams. *Bright Morning*. The Viking Press, 1942.

Bianco, Margery Williams. *The Little Wooden Doll*. Macmillan Publishing Co., Inc., 1953.

Bianco, Margery Williams. *Poor Cecco: The Wonderful Story of a Wonderful Wooden Dog Who Was the Jolliest Toy in the House until He Went out to Explore the World*. George H. Doran Company, 1925.

Bianco, Margery Williams. *The Skin Horse*. Green Tiger Press, 1978.

Bianco, Margery Williams. *The Velveteen Rabbit*. Doubleday & Company, Inc., 1922.

Bianco, Margery Williams. *Winterbound*. Dover Publications, 2014.

Bianco, Pamela. *Paradise Square*. Oxford University Press, 1950.

de la Mare, Walter. *Songs of Childhood*. Krill Press, 2015.

Koplow, Lesley. *Bears Bears Everywhere!* Teachers College Press, 2008.

Koplow, Lesley. Email message, Emotionally Responsive Schools Conference, Oct–Nov 2021.

Mahony, Bertha Miller and Anne Carroll Moore, eds. *Writing and Criticism: A Book for Margery Bianco*. The Horn Book, Inc., 1951.

Poem Hunter. "Margery Williams—Margery Williams Biography—Poem Hunter." www.poemhunter.com/margery-williams/biography.

Wood, J. G. *Natural History*. George Rutledge and Sons, 1894.